D1214337

VINTAGE POST CARDS OF NEW YORK

from

THE STEFANO AND SILVIA LUCCHINI COLLECTION

STEFANO AND SILVIA LUCCHINI

UNIVERSE

A WALK THROUGH OLD NEW YORK

Imagine perusing a local estate auction and among the various objects and art a small and worn wooden box catches your eye. You open it and inside you find a world of memories and history and storytelling in the most miniature form: the postcard. The beauty and nostalgia of this collection of old postcards from New York lies in the fact that it is so intimate. It tells of travel and living, of friendships and family and love, and of the stuff New York is made on. So by opening that box you are transported to a different time and place. Your imagination is drawn in to the bygone days of New York, where the buildings soar above you and the people bustle about in the crowded streets, where history oozes from the sidewalks and culture greets you at every corner. This collection gives us the chance to marvel, as generations past have marveled, at the character and greatness that is New York - a melting pot city that has been home to some of the world's most fascinating people, and a place where just about anything is possible. The collected experiences of these forgotten postcards invite us to discover the vibrancy and grandeur, the history and humanity of what was then and still remains one of the greatest cities in the world.

MIDTOWN

CENTRAL PARK

IN THE EARLY 1930S, CENTRAL PARK CERTAINLY HAD ITS PE-CULIARITIES. ONE COULD TAKE A ROWBOAT OUT ONTO THE lake for a romantic afternoon, or a stroll to Sheep Meadow where sheep actually grazed out in the open. But just north, at the Central Park Reservoir, which had recently been emptied, one would find something quite different: a "Hooverville," or shantytown, where hundreds of displaced workers and families camped out after the stock market crash of 1929. It was Robert Moses, New York's master city planner, who in 1934 stepped in to turn Central Park into the oasis it has become today, with ball parks and playgrounds, theater performances and concerts, and of course, the Great Lawn, a vast green pasture that replaced the Central Park Reservoir.

THE TERRACE

BOATHOUSE

Entrance to Central Park, New York

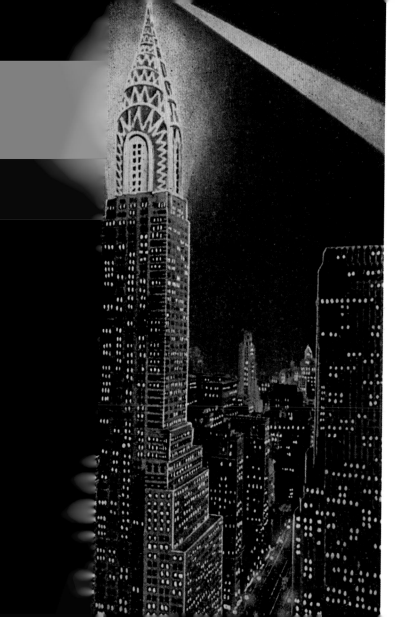

THE CHRYSLER
BUILDING

O F ALL THE BUILDINGS IN THE NEW YORK CITY SKY-
LINE, PERHAPS THE MOST ICONIC IS THE CHRYSLER
Building. Completed less than a year after the stock
market crash of 1929, it is a stainless steel ode to progress and
resilience. Its ribbed and layered geometrical crown is a glittering reminder of the Statue of Liberty and the freedom and
opportunity it represents. With its spire and needle rocketing
to the sky, its height surpassed even that of the Eiffel Tower,
securing its title as the tallest building in the world. But New
York City in the 1920s and '30s was an architectural battlefield,
and the Chrysler Building would soon be trumped by its adver-
sary, the Empire State Building.

1A:—CHRYSLER BUILDING, NEW YORK CITY

UNIVERSAL POSTAL UNION
Union Postale Universelle
UNITED STATES OF AMERICA
ÉTATS-UNIS D'AMÉRIQUE

THIS SIDE IS FOR ADDRESS ONLY

POSTAL CARD — CARTE POSTALE

U.S. POSTAGE
TWO CENTS

Le 29 Mars 1900.

NEW YORK, N.Y.
MAR 22
7-PM
1931

GRAND CENTRAL STATION

CENTRAL STATION, NEW YORK.

Herald Square, New York

HERALD SQUARE

T HE BUSY INTERSECTION OF BROADWAY, 34TH STREET AND 6TH AVENUE, BETTER KNOWN AS HERALD Square, was once home to New York's most sensational newspaper, *The New York Herald*. Its founder, James Gordon Bennett, Sr., was once quoted as saying that a newspaper is meant "not to instruct, but to startle," and the *Herald* did just that. The building that housed the newspaper was completed in 1894 and topped with a large bronze statue of Minerva, goddess of wisdom. Below her, two mechanized typesetters wearing printers' aprons would swing their mallets into a bell that marked the time. When the building was demolished in 1921, this statue was placed in what is now known as Herald Square, where the two typesetters still mark the time for the thousands of New Yorkers passing by.

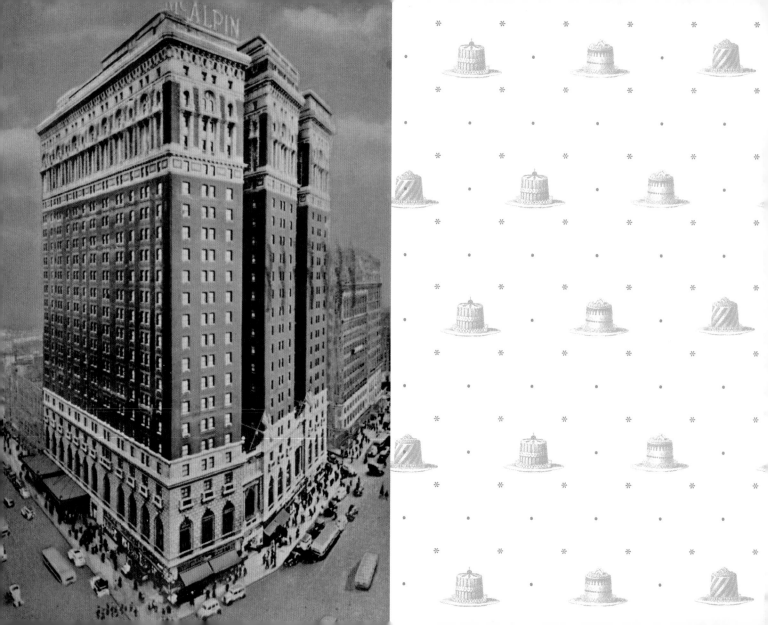

THE SHERATON-McALPIN HOTEL

SIMONE DE BEAUVOIR ONCE WROTE "THERE IS SOME-THING IN THE NEW YORK AIR THAT MAKES SLEEP useless," supporting the old adage that New York is a city that never sleeps. Though sleep may feel useless in New York, a hotel room certainly did not for the millions of visitors pouring into the city at the turn of the century. In 1912, the Sheraton-McAlpin Hotel opened its doors to the public and impressed New Yorkers and visitors alike with its twenty-five stories and 1,500 guest rooms. A *New York Times* article celebrating its opening declares in its headline that there are separate floors for men, women and night workers. Rising high above the bustle and ruckus of 34th Street and Broadway, the McAlpin was the perfect place to get some sleep, or at least some peace and quiet.

THE WALDORF ASTORIA

A T THE TURN OF THE CENTURY, DINING OUT WAS ALL THE RAGE FOR MANHATTAN'S ELITE. MEN IN tails and top hats, ladies in gowns and furs, and the city's biggest names would wait to be seated at New York's most coveted tables to revel in the gastronomical and musical entertainment of the Waldorf Astoria's lavish ballrooms and lounges. It was a high society stomping ground and *the place* to be and be seen. It defined an era of New York aristocracy and continues to set the standard of luxury and class for New York City hotels.

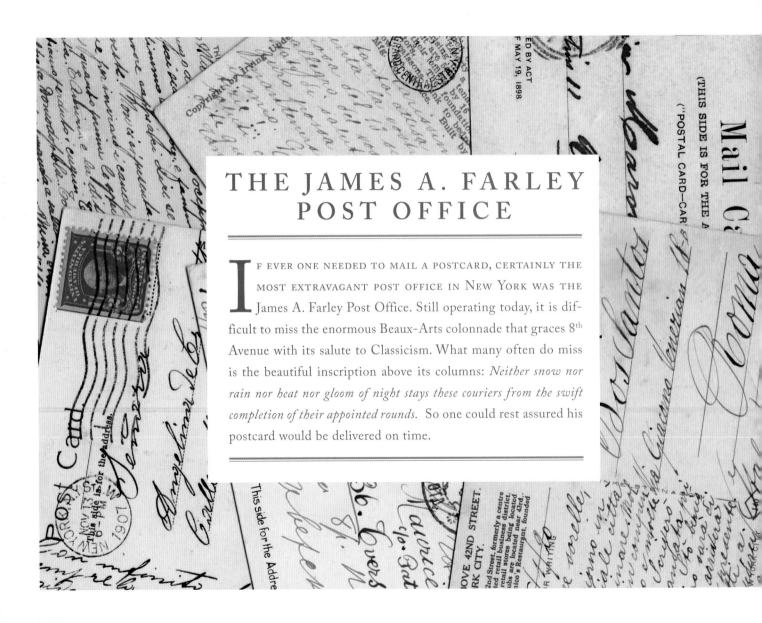

THE JAMES A. FARLEY
POST OFFICE

I F EVER ONE NEEDED TO MAIL A POSTCARD, CERTAINLY THE MOST EXTRAVAGANT POST OFFICE IN NEW YORK WAS THE James A. Farley Post Office. Still operating today, it is difficult to miss the enormous Beaux-Arts colonnade that graces 8th Avenue with its salute to Classicism. What many often do miss is the beautiful inscription above its columns: *Neither snow nor rain nor heat nor gloom of night stays these couriers from the swift completion of their appointed rounds.* So one could rest assured his postcard would be delivered on time.

New General Post Office, New York City.

NEW YORK CITY

PHOTO BY GOTTSCHO

ROCKEFELLER CENTER

O<small>N</small> C<small>HRISTMAS</small> E<small>VE</small>, 1931, <small>A GROUP OF WEARY</small> <small>CONSTRUCTION WORKERS RALLIED AROUND A</small> very large Christmas tree decorated with tinsel and garlands and pushed it into place. They had cause to celebrate, for on that night they were to receive their pay-check, and so began the tradition of the renowned Rocke-feller Center Christmas tree. At a time when America was deeply mired in the Great Depression, Rockefeller Center's construction, financed almost entirely by J. D. Rockefeller, employed over 40,000 people. The 22-acre complex contains over a dozen commercial buildings, a large central plaza, an ice-skating rink and one of the most beloved entertainment halls of New York City, Radio City Music Hall. Yet Rockefeller Center is not simply a group of buildings; it is J. D. Rockefeller's microcosmic vision, a city within a city, a meeting place, a community, and a dynamic landmark of tradition and art.

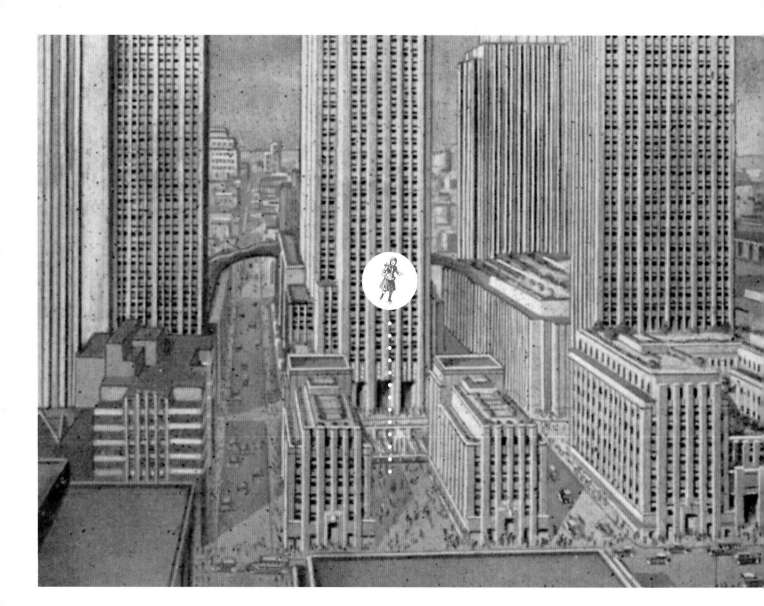

ST. PATRICK'S CATHEDRAL

5TH AVENUE IS THE BACKBONE OF NEW YORK'S RISE AND PROGRESS, boasting some of the city's most awe-inspiring landmarks, and among these is one of the oldest, St. Patrick's Cathedral. Its striking, Gothic beauty is now padded by high rises and department stores. However, in 1858, when the keystone was finally laid, 5th Avenue and 50th Street was not the bustling commercial center that it is now. One can only imagine, then, how majestic and distinguished St. Patrick's was when its spires were completed in 1888. Though it may not have seemed so tall in the 1920s, when 5th Avenue solidified its status as a high-end shopping district, its spires were no less magnificent.

St. Patrick's Cathedral, New York

SUNDAY MORNING ON 5TH AVE., NEW YORK CITY.

THE TIMES
BUILDING

Times Building.
New York City.

In 1905, *The New York Times* moved its headquarters to the corner building of 7th Avenue, Broadway and 42nd Street, soon to be known as One Times Square. Though they would move out only eight years later, the newspaper owned the building until 1961 and continued to use it to inform the public of important events. Thousands of people would gather in the square to wait for instant news of boxing matches, baseball games, trials and wartime announcements, and in 1928, the building boasted its first electronic news ticker. Now completely covered from top to bottom with signage, screens and scrolling electronic news banners, it is still one of the most popular sites in New York, especially on New Year's Eve when millions of spectators await the famous ball drop from atop the building's flagpole.

Fifth Avenue, New York.

5ᵀᴴ AVENUE

I N THE LATE 19ᵀᴴ CENTURY, 5ᵀᴴ AVENUE WAS THE REALM OF NEW YORK'S OLDEST AND WEALTHIEST RESIDENTS. Socialites clad in bonnets and top hats would stroll down the boulevard on foot or by carriage, stopping to visit friends and family for tea and parties. New York, as Edith Wharton describes it in her novel *The Age of Innocence*, most of which takes place on 5ᵗʰ Avenue, "was a small and slippery pyramid, in which…hardly a fissure had been made or a foothold gained," yet this old-world society rooted in European aristocracy wouldn't last for long in light of the encroaching architectural, industrial and commercial boom that would eventually envelop and define 5ᵗʰ Avenue.

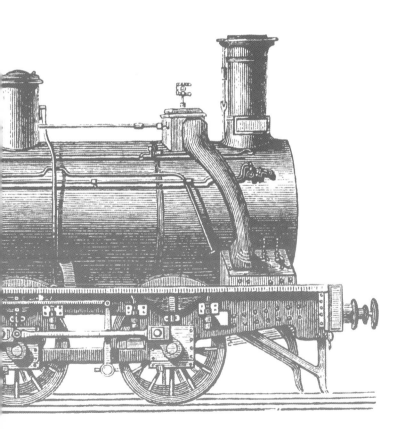

GRAND CENTRAL
STATION

HUNDREDS OF HURRIED COMMUTERS ZIGZAG ACROSS THE TENNESSEE MARBLE FLOOR, BRIEF-cases and travel bags in tow. Chatter fills the gi-gantic main concourse and echoes from its walls while sun-light streams in rays through the high-set windows as passen-gers move from terminal to terminal. Families wait anxiously for loved ones, lovers share passionate farewells, and some simply stop to marvel at the extraordinary beauty and energy that is Grand Central Station. Completed in 1913, it was a pioneer of engineering, replacing steam technology with electricity and seamlessly connecting thousands of passen-gers and trains. In that same year, while gazing at the starry night sky depicted on the main concourse ceiling, a passenger noted that the constellations were painted backwards, which has never been explained.

New Grand Central Terminal Station, New York.

MADISON SQUARE PARK

THIS LOVELY PARK HAS SEEN SO MUCH DE-
VELOP AND EVOLVE AROUND IT SINCE ITS
birth in 1847. Its trees have long shad-
ed New Yorkers from the sweltering sun and its
lawns and paths and monuments have given them
a peaceful meeting place. So in 1901, when a Lon-
don businessman attempted to replace the park's
benches with cushioned rocking chairs available by
payment only, New Yorkers fought back and won,
confirming the solidarity and sense of community
on which the city was built.

Madison Square
Garden,
New York City.

DOWNTOWN

THE FLATIRON
BUILDING

U PON ITS COMPLETION IN 1902, THE FLATIRON
BUILDING WAS QUITE THE CONTROVERSY. NOT
only did it stand out as New York's second sky-
scraper, but its wedge shape, the "flat iron" as locals called
it, was both innovative and modern. It became an object of
fascination for artists, photographers and writers alike, rep-
resenting progress and forward thinking, strong and proud in
its novel features. When photographer Alfred Stieglitz saw
the finished building for the first time he noted that it "ap-
peared to be moving toward [him] like the bow of a monster
ocean steamer - a picture of new America still in the mak-
ing," and indeed it was just that.

Madison Square

Flatiron Building, N. Y. City

UNION SQUARE

UNION SQUARE HAS ALWAYS BEEN ONE OF THE GREAT MEETING PLACES OF NEW YORK CITY. LOCATED at the intersection of Broadway and 4th Avenue, the park is a union of two major avenues and the myriad people of New York. Here one could and still can gather with friends to sit on the green under the shade of trees in full bloom, or observe the steady stream of passersby shuffling down 14th Street from the steps of the park's entrance. In the midst of New York's concrete, angular grid, Union Square remains one of the most cherished public spaces in the city.

WASHINGTON SQUARE PARK

IN THE LATE 19TH CENTURY, THIS LOVELY AREA ATTRACTED SOME OF MANHATTAN'S WEALTHIEST residents who built homes along the brim of the park, and what made it particularly fashionable was its accessibility to carriages and automobiles. One could cruise down 5th Avenue, enter the park and circle its central fountain on large paved paths, or stop to observe its most striking feature, the Washington Arch, completed in 1892 in honor of the nation's first president. Henry James, in his short novel *Washington Square*, writes that the area "has a kind of established repose which is not of frequent occurrence in other quarters of the long, shrill city; it has a riper, richer, more honorable look…" – an opinion still upheld by many.

THE FINANCIAL DISTRICT

WHILE MEANDERING THROUGH THE OFTEN NARROW STREETS OF NEW YORK'S FINANCIAL district one can feel history pulsing in the movement and buildings, the cobblestones and monuments. It is here where traders in the 18th century formed the original New York Stock Exchange; where the first president of the United States, George Washington, was inaugurated; where the financial giants J. P. Morgan and J. D. Rockefeller centered their industries; where Charles H. Dow first began analyzing stocks. The innovations, advancements and tumbles that would occur in this center of finance would change the face of American, and even global history.

Municipal Building,
Newspaper Row and City Hall Park,
New York City.

City Hall, New York City.

CITY HALL AND MUNICIPAL BUILDING OF NEW YORK

S OMETHING ABOUT LOWER MANHATTAN FEELS DIFFERENT FROM THE REST OF THE CITY. ITS EARLY AMERICAN, COLONIAL TONES ARE SOMEWHAT OLDER, MORE HISTORIC and reminiscent of America's provenance and infancy. Take a walk down Park Row and stop on Broadway to admire the oldest city hall in America, completed in 1812. Originally, New York was a major contestant in the running for America's civic center, and for a period after the Revolutionary War it was, in fact, the official seat of American government.

WALL STREET

I N THE EARLY 1600S, DUTCH SETTLERS ERECTED A WOODEN BARRICADE ALONG THE NORTHERN BOUNDARY of their settlement, presumably to thwart any attacks from British and Native American forces. When British colonialists took over, the barricade was eventually torn down and the space below it was paved into what would become Wall Street. Initially a trading and meeting place for local businessmen, this street would become the very heart of American economy and finance – a testament to some of the proudest and most devastating moments in the nation's history.

St. Paul's Chapel, New York City.

TRINITY CHURCH & ST. PAUL'S CHAPEL

To STAND BEFORE EITHER OF THESE CHURCHES IS TO STAND BEFORE A HISTORICAL MONUMENT. BOTH St. Paul's Chapel and Trinity Church are part and parcel of America's rocky departure from Colonial England and have stood witness to the birth of American democracy. George Washington was inaugurated at St. Paul's Chapel and his chief of staff and fellow founding father, Alexander Hamilton, was buried in the Trinity churchyard. So among the rising skyscrapers and haste of a growing financial district, the beautiful St. Paul's Chapel and Trinity Church offered commuters and passersby a moment's refuge and a reminder of the great history that lay in these city blocks.

BROADWAY

In a way, Broadway is the central artery of New York, thriving with life and movement, without which the city would simply unravel. It is also the island's oldest thoroughfare running North to South, originally paved in dirt by the native Lenape people. Since then, it has stood witness to the city's great expansion and growth, evolution and rise. Its passage is essential to the very vitality of the city, not excluding the electric lights that lit up the street in the 1890s, or the yellow stream of taxis and their honking horns, or the masses bobbing up and down its sidewalks. Broadway has seen it all – from the razing of the forests to the rise of New York's new and ever-evolving landscape, but amidst this change, it has always remained a constant, nurturing bedrock of the city.

THE ST. PAUL BUILDING

THIS STOCKY, CLASSICAL BUILDING ONCE ROSE TWENTY-SIX STORIES OVER BROADWAY AND ANNE Street, just across the street from St. Paul's Chapel where it gets its name. Completed in 1898, it was one of the tallest buildings in the city. The *New York Times* even referred to it as "towering" over other buildings in a 1911 article; yet as the city forged into the 20th century, Beaux-Arts architecture became less relevant in a more progressive, cutting-edge architectural field. In 1958, the building was razed to the ground and replaced by the Western Electric building, and such was the fate of so many of New York's lost architectural gems.

THE WOOLWORTH BUILDING & THE SINGER BUILDING

AMERICAN AUTHOR JOHN STEINBECK ONCE WROTE THAT NEW YORK "ISN'T LIKE THE REST OF THE country... Littleness gets swallowed up here," which was especially true during the early 20th century's race for the sky. The now demolished Singer Building, completed in 1908, and the Woolworth Building, completed in 1913, were towering examples of the ambition and architectural grandeur of New York. Upon its completion, the Singer Building was the world's tallest building, quickly surpassed by its neighbor, the Woolworth Building, which remains among New York's architectural treasures.

City Prison, (The Tombs)
New York City.

NEW YORK CITY PRISON
(The Tombs)

IN THE EARLY HALF OF THE 19TH CENTURY, THE CENTRAL PART OF LOWER MAN-HATTAN WAS KNOWN AS THE FIVE POINTS SLUM, A BREEDING GROUND FOR DISEASE, destitution and violent crime. In 1838, a prison modeled after an Egyptian mausoleum was built upon a rank collect pond, and it eventually began to sink into the fetid mire. The jail was replaced by a new structure in 1902 that connected it to the courthouse across the street. The "Bridge of Sighs," named after its Venetian predecessor, is where prisoners would take in their last glimpse of daylight before going into the jail that is still known today as The Tombs.

CASTLE CLINTON

BATTERY PARK

Looking out onto the ocean from Battery Park feels as if you are standing at the edge of the world. There is a sense of openness and airiness that cannot be felt in any other part of the city, where high-rises and skyscrapers obstruct most views of the horizon as mountains would. Initially, the park served as an artillery battery, hence its name, and would eventually become America's first receiving center for immigrants.

Its most impressive feature is certainly Castle Clinton, which served as a military fort until 1821.

Greetings from the Greater New York

NEW YORK HARBOR

In the thick of the city, among the mountainous skyscrapers and valleys of avenues, it is easy to forget that New York is, in fact, an island flanked by two major rivers with its southernmost tip hemmed in by one of the most important ports on the East Coast. At the turn of the century, New York Harbor swelled with ocean liners and tugboats, sails and masts and steam, with ships unloading and loading their stock, with mariners and merchants, fish markets and maritime pubs. It was a chaotic hub of commerce that played a crucial role in the development of New York City.

BEYOND
MANHATTAN
ISLAND

BROOKLYN BRIDGE

IN THE LATE 19TH CENTURY, NO ONE CAPTURED NEW YORK BETTER THAN THE TRANscendental poet and native Brooklynite, Walt Whitman. In his poem *Crossing Brooklyn Ferry*, he describes the sights and sounds of the East River and "the hundreds and hundreds that cross, returning home…" on the Brooklyn ferryboats. So in 1878, when he returned to his home city and saw the nearly finished Brooklyn Bridge, he wrote that it had been "the most effective medicine my soul has yet partaken… namely, Manhattan Island and Brooklyn, which the future shall join in one city—city of superb democracy, amid superb surroundings."

THE BROOKLYN RAIL

FOR THE AVERAGE NEW YORKER, GETTING AROUND THE CITY IN THE 19TH CENTURY WITHOUT A HORSE OR CARriage could be quite tricky, and with Brooklyn's growing population and fashionable tourist destinations like Coney Island, public transportation became a major point of concern. Various railroad companies began building elevated train lines in Brooklyn, Manhattan and Queens, and with the help of the Brooklyn and Williamsburg Bridges, they were able to run trolley and train services connecting the boroughs. No longer dependent on the Brooklyn Ferry, commuters would pack onto tram cars and cross the East River, returning home if not more comfortably, then at least more easily.

THE STATUE
OF LIBERTY

IMAGINE REACHING THE END OF A LONG AND WEARY TRANSATLANTIC VOYAGE ON AN OVERCROWDED SHIP CARrying thousands of immigrants and looking up to see a golden giant rising out of the ocean, with broken chains at her feet and a torch lifted high above her crowned head, and knowing that you had made it. To see the Statue of Liberty through the eyes of a 19th-century immigrant is to really understand the power of its symbolism. Completed in 1884, Lady Liberty was a gift from the French intended to commemorate the centennial of the Declaration of Independence and the alliance that America and France had forged since then. In 1883, Emma Lazarus gave voice to what would become America's beacon of freedom in her poem *The New Colossus*: "Give me your tired, your poor, your huddled masses yearning to breathe free."

ELLIS ISLAND

In 1892, a "New York Times" article announced the first entrance of an immigrant into Ellis Island: "A rosy-cheeked Irish girl the first registered-room enough for all arrivals." It boasted of the island's superb organization and ability to disembark and process thousands of people in a relatively short amount of time. While first and second-class passengers were received directly at New York Harbor, those with third-class tickets were brought to Ellis Island for legal questioning and medical examinations. Though this often required long lines and tight quarters, most were happy to be on the ground after weeks on overcrowded and poorly equipped steamboats. Over twelve million people would enter America through this landing depot, which would soon become the symbol of turn-of-the-century American immigration.

Williamsburg Bridge, New York

WILLIAMSBURG
BRIDGE

TO
GRAND ST

FERRY ON THE HUDSON RIVER

Subway Car, Brooklyn

CURVED
ELEVATED
RAILWAY

Elevated R. R. Curve at 110th Street, New York.

Copyright by A. Loe
Tompkinsville, N.

THE HARLEM RIVER
SPEEDWAY

In 1898, a wide, unpaved speedway, nowadays known as the Harlem River Drive, opened along the west bank of the Harlem River, accessible to horses and carriages only. This made for a sort of elite playing field, where sportsmen would hold equestrian races and spectators would gather to observe regattas and boat races on the pedestrian paths that flanked the central roadway. This quaint, country-like haven would retain its charm until 1919 when it was finally opened to traffic.

QUEENSBORO BRIDGE

I N THE 19ᵀᴴ CENTURY, MANY OF MANHATTAN'S WEALTHI-
EST RESIDENTS BEGAN TO BUILD LARGE ESTATES IN THE
lush terrain of Queens and Long Island where they would
escape for the weekend or the summer. It is very fitting, then,
that the narrator of *The Great Gatsby*, a novel set on the pros-
perous Long Island of the 1920s, so perfectly expresses that
"the city seen from the Queensboro Bridge is always the city
seen for the first time, in its first wild promise of all the mystery
and the beauty in the world."

New York City.

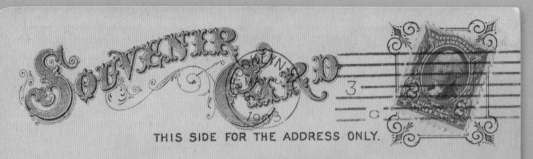

THIS SIDE FOR THE ADDRESS ONLY.

J UST UNDER THE HELL GATE BRIDGE LIES A NARROW STRAIT OF VIOLENT TIDAL WATERS THAT HAS SEEN MANY A SHIP SINK BELOW ITS CHOPPY, SWIRLING SURFACE. Perhaps the most famous shipwreck was that of the 28-gun British Revolutionary War frigate Hussar, that allegedly went down in 1780 with nearly one million pounds of British gold on board. Over the years, many have attempted to find the lost gold, including Thomas Jefferson, through expensive and complex expeditions, but as luck would have it, the mystery of the Hussar's sunken treasure remains buried in the murky bed of the East River.

HELL GATE

CASTLE WILLIAMS

Just about half a mile away from Battery Park, right in the middle of the East River, is Governors Island, a lush expanse of green originally reserved for the British Royal governors of New York. In 1807, the Army Core of Engineers built Castle Williams, a defensive structure that would function as a U.S. military prison until the 1960s. Though the island may have seemed obsolete to the average passerby, it was actually a functioning Coast Guard base until 1997.

Bird's Eye View
of Luna Park,
Coney Island, N. Y.

CONEY ISLAND: LUNA PARK

I N THE SEARING HEAT OF NEW YORK CITY SUMMERS, CROWDS WOULD POUR ONTO CONEY ISLAND BEACHES, and with the opening of Luna Park in 1903, Coney Island became a place of magic and wonder, electric and alive. At night, Luna Park lit up its Arabian towers with over 250,000 lights. At the turn of the century, such a sight was truly remarkable. "Everything glitters, totters, teeters, titters," wrote Henry Miller of Coney Island, and you could have it all for just a nickel.

CONEY ISLAND: SURF AVENUE

SURF AVENUE WAS CONEY ISLAND'S MAIN THOROUGH-FARE, LINED WITH CAROUSELS, RESTAURANTS, TENTS and towers, minarets, hot dog stands, scenic railway rides like Pike's Peak, and countless amusements for the swarming crowds passing by. It was New York's playground and it allowed for a special mixing of all the city's rank and class. "I see millionaires eatin' popcorn and trampin' along with the crowd; and I see eight-dollar-a-week clothin'-store clerks in red automobiles fightin' one another for who'd squeeze the horn when they come to a corner," observes Dennis Carnahan in O. Henry's short story *The Greater Coney*.

1964 NEW YORK WORLD'S FAIR

O F ALL THE PARKS TO VISIT IN NEW YORK CITY, MOST VISITORS DO NOT PUT FLUSHING MEADOWS in Queens high on their list, but in 1964 this park glistened with futuristic structures and sensational international pavilions all in the name of the World's Fair. It was the dawn of the space age, and the fair imagined the future of mankind and the world of tomorrow, symbolized by the Unisphere, a giant steel globe at the center of the park. The artifacts left behind, like the New York Pavilion's spacecraft-shaped observation towers, offer a glimpse into how the past envisioned the future, but beyond the modern fanfare, there was still time for some good old entertainment at the Ringling Brothers Circus.

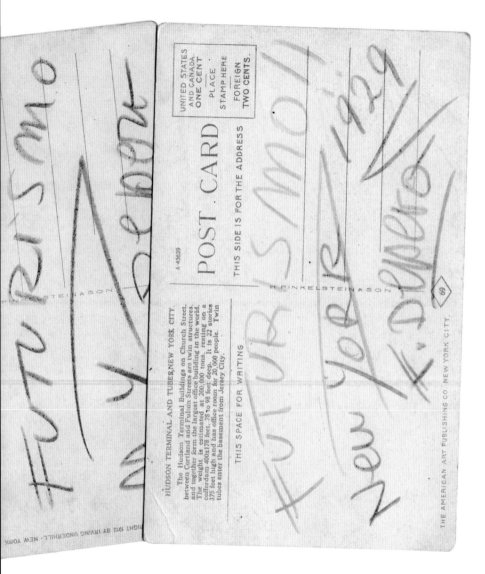

FORTUNATO DEPERO

THE BEDLAM OF ENGINES, TRAMS AND HORNS, THE PATTER AND TAPPING OF shoes on pavement, and the clanking of steel against steel are among some of the perpetual sounds of the raucous, skyrocketing New York of the 1920s. This all made for a sort of Futurist wonderland where industry and progress seemed at once grotesque and unstoppable. Fortunato Depero moved to New York in 1928 and was so taken with the city that he stayed for two years, experimenting in architecture, painting, media and theater. Depero wrote of the city that, "humanity is more manifold and colorful...tradition is a thing unknown [and] tomorrow is a magnet everybody wears on their nose," a seemingly perfect place for anyone with his eye on the future.

Hudson Terminal and Tubes, New York City.

Singer Building, and part of Financial District, New York City.

TIMES SQUARE BY

NEW YORK CITY OF THE FUTURE

CREATIVE THINKERS OF THE EARLY 20TH CENTURY WERE INSPIRED BY THE RAPID PROGRESS OF THE city that in 1913 Marcel Duchamp called "a complete work of art." Indeed, it was an age of visionary city planning and master engineering. The city radiated with steel towers and suspension bridges that boasted a host of superlative titles: tallest, strongest, longest, etc. Anything and everything felt possible and visions of the future were boundless. While living in New York, Fortunato Depero envisioned a quixotic aerial city, or what he called his "fantasy land," with "mechanical automatons, flying trains and fabulous flora and fauna; they travel through the leaden walls of skyscrapers, through the iron perspective of bridges and elevated trains… in the dense and asphyxiating air of the metropolis."

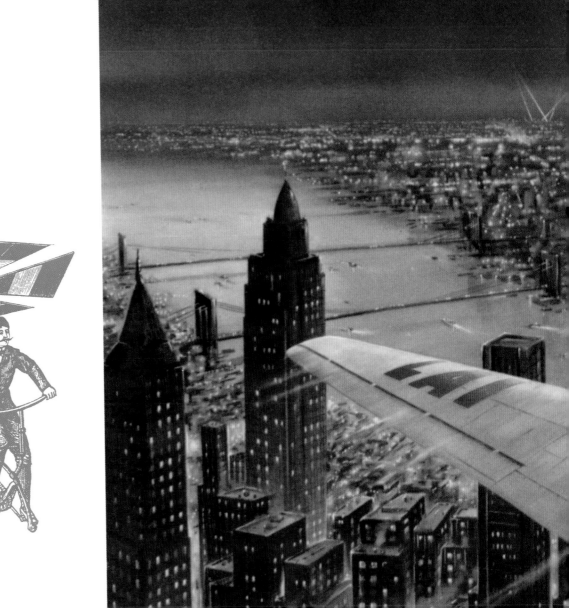

NEW YORKERS

LONG BEFORE THE ARRIVAL OF GIOVANNI DA VER-
RAZZANO AND HENRY HUDSON, MANHATTAN, OR
Mannahatta, the "land of many hills," was inhabited
by the native Lenape people. Though they would eventually
be pushed out by colonial forces, it is the ebb and flow of
this ever-changing city and the people who inhabit it that
lends it its humanity in all its flaws and triumphs. The sil-
very, glittering skyline, the myriad sights and sounds are truly
spectacular, but the real essence of New York, that indescrib-
able something, is its people, and to be a part of that, even
if just for a moment, is exhilarating. And so Walt Whitman
proclaims in his ode to his beloved city, Mannahatta, "A million people--manners free and superb--open voices--hospi-
tality--the most courageous and friendly young men, City of
hurried and sparkling waters! city of spires and masts! City
nested in bays! my city!"

ITALIAN BREAD PEDDLERS.

5690. COPYRIGHT, 1902, BY DETROIT PHOTOGRAPHIC CO.

N.Y. 7/4/02

PLACES

MIDTOWN

Central Park
The Chrysler Building
Herald Square
The Sheraton-McAlpin Hotel
The Waldorf Astoria
The James A. Farley Post Office
Rockefeller Center
St. Patrick's Cathedral
The Times Building
5th Avenue
Grand Central Station
Madison Square Park

DOWNTOWN

The Flatiron Building
Union Square
Washington Square Park
The Financial District
City Hall and Municipal Building of New York
Wall Street
Trinity Church and St. Paul's Chapel
Broadway

The St. Paul Building
The Woolworth Building and the Singer Building
New York City Prison (The Tombs)
Battery Park
New York Harbor

BEYOND MANHATTAN ISLAND

Brooklyn Bridge
The Brooklyn Rail
The Statue of Liberty
Ellis Island
Williamsburg Bridge
Curved Elevated Railway
The Harlem River Speedway
Queensboro Bridge
Hell Gate Bridge
Castle Williams
Coney Island: Luna Park
Coney Island: Surf Avenue
1964 New York World's Fair
Fortunato Depero
New York City of the Future
New Yorkers

POST CARD

First published in the United States of America in
2015 by Rizzoli International Publications, Inc.
300 Park Avenue South
New York, NY 10010
www.rizzoliusa.com

Originally published in Italian as Forgotten Postcards
of New York
© 2013 RCS Libri S.p.A.
All rights reserved
www.rizzoli.eu

Text Alyce Aldige
Art Direction Francesca Leoneschi
Book Design and Typesetting
Mauro De Toffol / *the*World*of*DOT

All rights reserved. No part of this book may
be reproduced, stored in a retrieval system,
or transmitted, in any form or by any means,
electronic, mechanical, photocopying, recording,
or otherwise, without prior consent of the
publishers.

2015 2016 2017 2018 / 10 9 8 7 6 5 4 3 2 1

ISBN: 978-0-8478-4536-1

Library of Congress Control Number: 2014948135

Printed in China

PLACE
STAMP HERE

One Cent Stamp
for United States
Canada & Mexico

Two Cent Stamp
for all other
countries

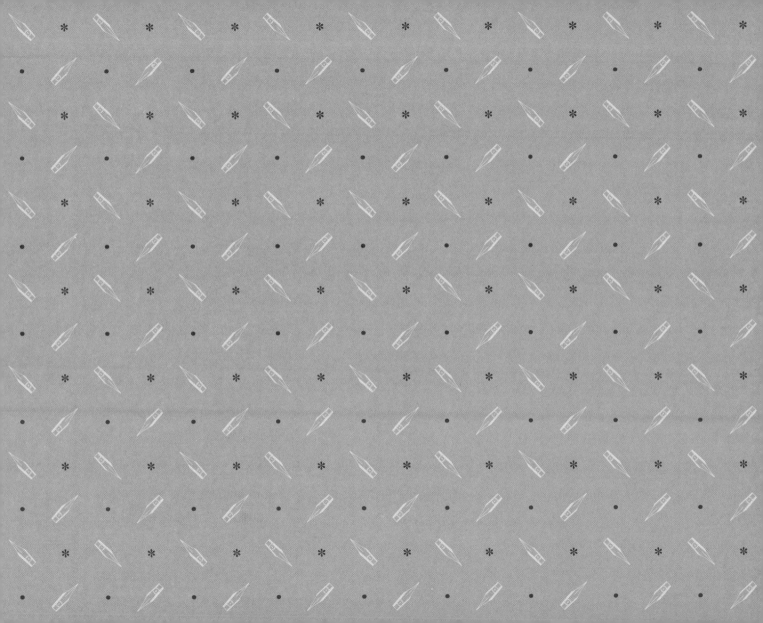